A 30-DAY DEVOTIONAL FOR FRESHMEN

FRESHMAN

MAKING FAITH YOUR PRIORITY

LARS ROOD

simply for students

YouthMinistry.com/TOGETHER

Freshman
Making Faith Your Priority

© 2013 Lars Rood

group.com
simplyyouthministry.com

Credits
Author: Lars Rood
Executive Developer: Nadim Najm
Chief Creative Officer: Joani Schultz
Editor: Rob Cunningham
Cover Art and Production: Veronica Preston

ISBN   978-0-7644-9002-6

10 9 8 7 6 5 4   20 19 18 17 16 15

Printed in the U.S.A.

TO KYLE AND PRESTON:

God brought us together your freshman year in that small group. You both know you drove me nuts. But I wouldn't change those memories for anything. We did more wrestling and fighting than talking about Jesus, but somehow he showed up and did some amazing things in your lives. I am so proud of who you have both become.

CONTENTS

INTRODUCTION

OK, I get it—you are a little bit freaked out. The last year of your life, you were at the top of the school. You were the oldest class, high on the pecking order of power and privilege. You were a big eighth-grader. But now you are getting ready to start over. For some of you that's a welcome thing. You are excited to leave the painful years of middle school behind and start fresh in a new school with new people. Maybe the last couple of years have been rough and you didn't have a good time. This is a chance for you to make your mark and decide you are going to be someone different or do something different. But you are a little scared because you really don't want it to be like the last few years. Others of you may have had a great time in junior high and you are just hoping that high school will continue that. But how do you make sure that will happen? What if it doesn't? You are worried that you don't really know what you are getting yourself into.

And faith is something that is important to you. You feel that there is this piece of your life that just seems more right when God is involved. It's hard to explain, but you know deep down that you want to stay close to him.

But you are making this big transition, and with all transitions, some things come with you and others are left behind. If you've ever moved houses you know what this feels like. You have to choose how important all your stuff is and make decisions based on that. Some things go in the truck, and others just get sold at a garage sale or are donated to charity.

The goal of this devotional is to help you think about your faith. You may have a great and strong faith that has been nurtured for years by loving parents, youth workers, church members, friends, coaches, and many other people. Or maybe it's been the opposite experience for you: You don't have a big community of Christ-followers around you that have been helping you grow. You've been doing it all on your own. Whatever your story, I believe this devotional series is for you. This book contains 30 different things for you to read, think, and pray about—plus action steps aimed at helping these ideas solidify a little bit more in your brain.

Your freshman year is an important one. It sets the stage for the rest of your high school time. You're going to experience so many things for the first time, and you'll benefit from thinking through how you want to respond in situations. It's our hope (meaning the collective world of adults who pray for you and desire to watch you make great decisions) that you would really figure out this year how to make faith your priority.

I'm not going to lie to you: It will not be easy. With this new season in your life you are going to have to deal with so many different things. I didn't do it perfectly. In fact I was probably a great example of imperfection. But what I did do right was to try to always prioritize my life so that faith never was too far in my back seat.

So my challenge to you is to try it out. This book probably won't change your life all by itself. But I hope it'll point out to you some steps and things that will help you as you work on figuring out how to be a ninth-grader who is trying to make your faith a priority.

How this book works:

This devotional includes 30 short things for you to think about. For each reading you'll find some sort of story and some follow-up questions to consider. You can do these by yourself, but you also can benefit from discussing them with a small group of people. This book might become 30 weeks of curriculum or simply provide 30 days of focus before the school year starts.

Each devotion includes a section called "The World Thinks." Most often these are comments that I have heard from non-Christians about these particular topics or issues. I don't hold back, so they may come across as a little negative. That's OK. You'll hear negative things all the time about your faith. The point is to encourage you to think through what people say and work out how you might respond to the thoughts and reactions people have about your faith in Christ.

You'll also find an action step for each devotion that is exactly what it sounds like: an opportunity to actually do something to discover and apply key truths. Often these are things that take some effort to accomplish and can help you grow. I want to encourage you to really put effort into doing them. Finally, I've included some Bible passages for you to look up—sometimes several, but usually just one or two. I want you to go deeper and explore other places in the Bible with more thoughts, stories, truths, and ideas that will help you.

It's my hope and prayer that these devotions will challenge you, encourage you, and put you in places where you will have the opportunity to make faith your priority.

SECTION 1

A WHOLE YEAR OF FIRSTS

Welcome to the first time you do a whole bunch of things! That's one of the great and scary things about your freshman year. You get to experience everything for the first time. Maybe this isn't a big deal because you handle change and transitions well. Or maybe you are a bit nervous about what this all means. The thing about firsts is that you only have one chance to experience them. For example, with a "first impression," you have really only one opportunity to show people who you are— and after that you are either reinforcing or trying to change what they think of you.

With all of these things you are stepping into brand-new territory. How will you respond? Do you have a plan? Are you prepared when things don't go the way you expected? Think and pray through these ideas. It's my goal to help you think about these "firsts" in the context of your faith journey. You might read that last sentence and say, "I don't have a faith journey." That's actually totally OK because the goal of this is to encourage you to consider things in a "new" way.

NO.1 THE FIRST DAY

You wake up. You put on some clothes. You grab something to eat and then head to school. You might be walking, getting dropped off, or catching a bus. It's a new school and you are feeling a bit nervous. Even if you don't want to admit it to yourself, it's affecting you. We have all been there. That feeling you get walking on campus for the first time can be scary. And guess what? That's OK. You are supposed to be feeling these things. It's natural and normal. But that probably doesn't make you feel better.

So how can the words in this devotional help you prepare? I'm going to let you in on a secret: They can't. The words in this book by themselves aren't going to give you any secrets to making it a better day. That's not the point of this book. There is no quick fix to making this year amazing. In fact, if you don't already know it, this year is probably going to be tough. But that's actually OK because you are going to learn a ton and grow in the midst of it.

Of course, now you are wondering what you are possibly going to learn if I've already told you my words are pretty useless. Well, that's the deal. You have to choose to actually do something with these words. Why don't you try it out right now?

You walk on campus and you have a choice. Who are you going to be? I don't know the condition of your faith. It might already be super strong, and that's amazing. But even if you have a strong faith, you still have to choose what to do with it and what it means to you. So here's what I want you to do. Open your eyes really big and see if for a brief moment of that first walk on campus you can see things as

Jesus might. That's going to take really only one thing: You have to move beyond yourself and think about everyone else. Not what they think about you but what you imagine they might be thinking.

THINK ABOUT:

1. How might Jesus want you to reach out to hurting people at your school? (Yes, as a freshman you can still have an impact.)

2. Do you want your faith to be a part of your life at school this year? Why or why not?

3. What things do you want to "bring" with you from your last school, and what things do you want to "leave" behind?

THE WORLD THINKS:

I'm pretty sure the world just wants you to leave your faith at church and not bring it to school. The big way the world wants to discourage you from thinking about Jesus at school is by making it seem weird. The world wants you to think that the two things don't go together and that if you want to try, you'll have to carry around a big Bible with you and preach in the lunchroom.

ACT:

Guess what? You can be a teenager who has faith and trust in Jesus without coming across as "weird." You don't have to carry a big Bible or preach on campus. What you need to do is pretty simple. In the Bible, Jesus talks a lot about loving people. What if you just decided this week that you were going to work on doing that? You could be the freshman who decides to talk to people that others seem to forget or ignore. You could choose to not talk bad about people. You could encourage your friends and tell people what you like about them. Why don't you go ahead and try that?

READ:

John 13:34 — think about how you could love people this week

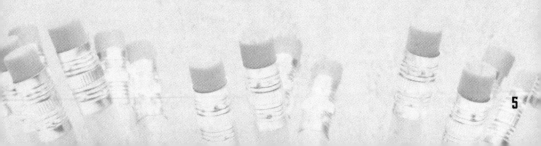

℠2 THE FIRST TEMPTATIONS

One of the main differences between middle school and high school is the amount of freedom that you have. This might depend upon your school, but you likely will have more opportunities in high school to be in places where temptations are in front of you than you did in junior high. And chances are good, too, that you might at some point be around some older friends who have experienced those things before you. Trust me when I say that there are just a lot more opportunities to get in trouble and to have things pop up in front of you that you haven't experienced before. Your faith can be super strong and a priority in your life, but if you haven't experienced some of these temptations before, how can you possibly be prepared?

The goal of this book is to help you make your faith a priority in your life. Here's a quick tip, though: It's really hard to make the right choice in the midst of temptation. In fact, I will go so far as to say that you will often fail if you find yourself having to make decisions when temptation is presented to you. But don't worry; there is hope! How? I encourage you to make the right choices *before* you enter tempting situations. That's the only way I know how to help you. As a freshman you need to figure out what you will do in situations way in advance. I hope you have some people in your life at church, youth group, in a small group, or just some friends that you can talk about how you want to react to temptation. I promise you that the work you do to talk through this ahead of time will absolutely help. Here's a bit of wisdom from my own bad experience. I didn't do enough preparation in high school, and I found myself getting into bad situations pretty regularly. I wish I could go back and think about how I wanted to respond in situations way before they happened.

THINK ABOUT:

1. How do you protect yourself from making bad choices?

2. What are some things that you know could potentially be major temptations to you?

3. How do temptations and struggle play into your faith journey?

THE WORLD THINKS:

You'll probably hear quite a few times this year that it's OK to experiment. The world will even tell you that many people make bad choices, but they all turn out OK, so you shouldn't feel bad if you struggle and stumble a little. *"Everyone is doing it,"* so it must be OK. You might even hear that your freshman year doesn't really matter, so if you are going to mess up, you should do it now. Adults might tell you that they all "experimented" a little, so it is OK if you want to do it.

ACT:

I don't want to be a major downer here, but if you want to really think about temptation and your faith, then you are going to have to ask people some hard questions. If you have some trusted adults in your life (yes, your parents can be in that category), I encourage you to ask them this hard question: "What did you do in high school that you wish you had never done or hadn't been tempted to do?" Yeah, I realize that's totally awkward and weird, but if your faith is something you want to grow, it's worth asking someone what he or she thinks.

READ:

Matthew 6:13, Luke 22:40, and 1 Corinthians 10:13

№3 THE FIRST PARTY

I'm pretty sure you will end up at your first party because (1) you got invited and decided to go or (2) you were with friends and next thing you knew, someone wanted to go to a party so you went along. Either way, how do you make some good choices about the way you are going to act? I remember the first party I went to. It was not a great decision on my part to go, and the entire time I knew I was somewhere I shouldn't have been, and I was worried I would get in trouble. I did make some good choices, though, and didn't partake in any of the illegal activities that happened there. One tough bit in all of this is that you might have a good time and maybe nothing bad happens. You might even have a great time. But sin and struggles have a way of slowly taking over our lives.

THINK ABOUT:

1. What do you think about drinking alcohol and getting drunk?

2. How confident do you feel saying no to something you don't want to do?

3. If you had to choose between being "popular" and a partier or "unpopular" and sober, which would you choose? Why?

THE WORLD THINKS:

You don't have to watch TV for too long to see people fully participating in the party lifestyle. The world wants you to believe that you can do that for a while and then simply stop and become a responsible adult. Look at the *Jersey Shore* phenomenon, where the whole show is about a group of young people drinking and partying for an entire summer. Next thing you know they are instant celebrities.

ACT:

What if there was something else for students to do on a Friday night instead of partying? I'm fairly certain that not every student's goal is to drink too much and puke. They just want to have fun. So how could you (or you and some friends) be a catalyst for fun? Do some brainstorming here and see if you can get some other people (maybe even adults) to help you pull off something that might be a fun evening.

READ:

2 Samuel 11–12 — watch the sin of David start affecting his life

№4 THE FIRST TESTS

As if you didn't already feel the pressure of having to "fit in" with the social world of your school, you now have to deal with the first academic parts of the year. You might face a lot of pressure from your parents to do well, which can be tough. Maybe you are totally scared because you really don't understand some of your classes. I remember the first test I bombed. My parents had pretty high expectations. I had a sister one year older than me who was an academic all-star. Unfortunately, I didn't understand my math class very well and I did horribly. I sat at home that night thinking that I was going to disappoint everyone once the scores came out. I had zero hope that I passed, and it really started me in a downward spiral of depression. But maybe that's not you. What if you feel super confident and comfortable going into your tests? That's a great place to be, too.

THINK ABOUT:

1. How do you study? Does it work well? Why or why not?

2. What classes do you feel confident in? Which ones do you struggle with?

3. You have the option to cheat and pass an exam, or not cheat but fail. What do you choose? Why?

THE WORLD THINKS:

"You are a freshman; what you do this year doesn't matter."
I've heard this over and over again from people. The world
wants you to just slide by and hide your struggles or try to find
ways to cheat and just get by. The world wants you to believe
that your struggles are not your fault and school is rigged
against you.

ACT:

Action in this area is relatively simple. Often when we don't
fully understand something, we find it really hard to ask for
help. And on the flipside, when we fully grasp something, we
often forget to think that others might benefit from our help.
So here's the action. If you are struggling, I encourage you
to ask for help. Talk to your teacher, another adult, another
student, or a counselor. Ask someone to help you. And if you
know what you're doing, look for someone who might need
your help. You have a gift that you could offer someone.

READ:

Exodus 17:2, Exodus 20:20, and 1 Chronicles 29:17

№5 THE FIRST DANCE

I hate dances. So remember that bias as you read the rest of this paragraph. I never missed a dance in high school. As much as I hated dancing and people watching me, I also didn't want to miss any part of the social scene. I went and stood on the wall with my friends. Talk about awkward! You might be very comfortable in those types of settings. But I'm guessing deep down you still have that nervous feeling as you wonder how you will fit in and if you will be accepted and liked. Dances can create a lot of anxiety, and chances are good that you've had the internal debate of wondering what you are doing there. I hope you have fun and can feel free. A quick reminder to give yourself: Chances are good that everyone feels just like you and no one is actually looking at you as intently as you are looking at yourself. So try to be free and enjoy. You don't have to dance, but it's always good for you to be yourself.

THINK ABOUT:

1. Who do you listen to that gives you value?

2. How comfortable are you in social settings such as a school dance? What do you fear—or enjoy?

3. What do you like to do? How can you do more of that?

THE WORLD THINKS:

In general it seems like the world values people who are different. So if you are "hyper social" or "slightly freaky," you have the most value in social settings. I think about MTV and *The Real World*. That show always has very interesting people, and I quickly realized after my application was rejected that I wasn't one of them. So you might not be getting any sort of encouragement to just be you. The world isn't probably going to encourage that.

ACT:

Figuring out who you are is difficult—especially if you are sitting around waiting for someone to tell you. Your action step is to take a "healthy risk" into something that is good and hard for you. That might mean having a difficult conversation with an adult or friend where you ask them to give them feedback about you. Or it might mean doing something as simple as stepping out on the dance floor and dancing with someone.

READ:

2 Samuel 6:1-22 and Luke 17:3-4

<small>NO.</small>6 THE FIRST FRIENDSHIPS

Roger was my first new friend of high school. We met the first day sitting side by side in band. We weren't friends in middle school but became pretty close in high school. It wasn't always easy to navigate new friendships in high school, but these friends felt a lot more "real" as I spent more time with them. During my freshman year, my parents let me hang out much more with friends independently from them. So, for example, my parents would drop us off at the movies instead of going with us. Roger and I became pretty close and ended up staying friends for a long time. But ultimately we lost touch with each other. I have great memories, though, of our time together. He was my friend, and I knew he liked me for who I was.

THINK ABOUT:

1. What types of qualities do you look for in a friend? Why?

2. How important is it for you to make deep friendships?

3. Do you have friends in your life that you can tell what you are truly feeling or thinking?

THE WORLD THINKS:

We are often taught that we need to be self-sufficient and that people can't be trusted. You might see depictions of friendships being fairly shallow on TV. Fortunately in this case, there are also some great solid long friendships that are also shown. This is one of those times where we need to follow the good examples from the world and try to not be self-sufficient and do things by ourselves.

ACT:

One thing I feel like I never tried in high school was reaching out to people who didn't fit into my perfect mold of friendship. As an adult I'm more and more open to becoming friends with people who are different from me. And God has been so good to bring a variety of people into my life. Your challenge: Go to school with an open mind and ask God who he would like you to spend time with. Then do it.

READ:

The best story of friendship I know from the Bible is the long-term relationship between David and Jonathan. It can be found in 1 Samuel 18–20. Jonathan's pledge to David is found in 1 Samuel 20:17.

NO.7 THE FIRST BIG ARGUMENT

You've probably had a few fights and arguments already in your life. Maybe they were with parents or siblings or close friends. Sadly, you will probably continue to encounter conflict in high school. But in high school it feels like the ramifications and consequences of arguments are so much worse. I can still remember the first major fight I had with a friend. He was mad at me because I didn't keep up my end of a plan to go work out each morning. It took a while for us to get over the dispute and for me to apologize. Fortunately, we are still friends, but it was one of those ugly moments.

THINK ABOUT:

1. How do you respond to conflict? Are you proud or ashamed of how you react? Why?

2. What are some strategies you could use to resolve some arguments? What things work for you?

3. What have you argued with your parents about? How can you more effectively handle those kinds of situations?

THE WORLD THINKS:

"You should always be right." One dominant philosophy in the world today is that you should never have to admit you were wrong. If someone doesn't like how you respond, just move on because that person is not worth the effort. Being right is more important than anyone else's feelings.

ACT:

More often than not we get into arguments because we don't fully try to understand and "hear" someone. Work on being a listener and repeating back to someone what they are saying, to show you are listening to them. I'll be the first to admit this isn't always easy, but it is so important in relationships and conflict.

READ:

Galatians 6:22-23 — think of the positive "fruit" that Paul talks about, and consider how focusing on these things can help you during arguments

NO.8 THE FIRST NEW DOUBTS

I want you to know that doubting is OK. Don't feel like you are weird or not a true Christ-follower if you have doubts. Teenagers who have grown up in the church are often frustrated because they feel like doubting is a sin or isn't OK. There was a season where I didn't feel like God was real in my life. I questioned internally a ton but never voiced those questions to anyone else. I didn't feel safe enough to share my thoughts at youth group or in church. I had been through confirmation, so that was supposed to seal it, right? But don't worry: God is bigger than your doubts.

THINK ABOUT:

1. Do you feel like doubting in God is safe? Why or why not?

2. Who in your life can you talk to when you have doubts?

3. How do you respond when you have doubts? Some people write, others pray, some talk, and others read. What works for you? Do it today!

THE WORLD THINKS:

The world is big on taking doubting to an extreme. In fact, we are often led to believe that we should doubt everything all the time. Doubt people's intentions. Doubt that there is any higher power. Doubt that you will make it or that anything will work out the way you want it to.

ACT:

What if you found a youth worker or trusted teacher and asked them to set up a "doubt" group? You could use cards to anonymously write your doubts and fears, or if you felt safe you could just share out loud. You could be honest and talk about the things you are having a hard time believing. You'd probably be surprised to find out you are not alone.

READ:

John 20:27 — Jesus was OK with even one of his disciples (Thomas) having doubts

NO.9 THE FIRST CRUSH

My first crush in high school was a girl named Donna. She was a year older than me and she had an orange Ford® Pinto. Donna was in my youth group, and we saw each other at school every day. As far as crushes go, this one was fairly harmless. We went to one dance and dated for only a couple of months. Nothing bad came out of it, and we had a pretty good friendship after that season as well. I think we were lucky, though. Donna and I dated back before cell phones, text messaging, the Internet, and all the other ways to stay connected. Because we weren't constantly connected, our relationship didn't grow very quickly. As a teenager today, you have the ability to be connected to people 24 hours a day if you want. It's so much harder than when I was young. But this means you probably really have to protect yourself.

THINK ABOUT:

1. Do you have a crush on someone? What things attract you, and what do you look for?

2. How have you seen crushes and dating go badly with your friends?

3. Do you think you are ready for a relationship now? Why or why not?

THE WORLD THINKS:

The world wants you to believe that simply jumping from one relationship to another is OK. You should "try out" a variety of different people so you will know what type of person you should be with. And the world wants you to believe that there aren't a lot of consequences to this type of dating. It's all about you anyway, right?

ACT:

Throw a party. Yes, a real party with guys and girls at it. But set it up to be safe for everyone. What if you got a group of friends together and did something fun that included interaction between guys and girls? Nothing serious like a dance or dates—just a fun night for people to interact, such as a bowling night or something like that. If you are in a youth group, maybe ask your youth leader for help. Think about people that you know might be struggling for friends. How can you be the type of friend that reaches out to them?

READ:

Genesis 29:16-28 — discover how Jacob loved Rachel

NO.10 THE FIRST BIG SUCCESS

Success is a funny thing. On one side is our desire to be proud of ourselves and feel like we accomplished something good. The other side, though, is that piece that makes us feel like we have to continue to replicate it in order to stand out. I imagine it's pretty tough to be an Olympic athlete. You have one chance every four years to compete for only a few medals. And most of the athletes only end up competing in the Olympics once in their whole lifetime. So, what if you went to the Olympics and won, but then that was the last win of your life? Yes, you would probably feel good, but in just a short while you probably wouldn't be as good, fast, or strong as you once were. The tension you have to deal with is how to enjoy the moment. God gives us gifts and talents, and we in turn have the opportunity to use them to glorify him.

THINK ABOUT:

1. What's one thing you know you are good at?

2. What types of successes have you had in the last six months? What about failures?

3. What have you learned from recent successes—and recent failures?

4. How does it feel when people around you are doing well but you aren't?

THE WORLD THINKS:

It sure seems the world says that people who have visible success are way more valuable than the rest of us. We see it all the time. Even at the Olympics, it's amazing to watch how much screen time is given to the athletes who have had constant success.

ACT:

How can you become the type of person that encourages others when they do something well? I'm not even talking about the easy encouragements when they win a race or achieve something great. What if you focused for a week on encouraging people who were doing things right in the day-to-day, mundane parts of life? How would it make someone feel if you encouraged that person for using kind words or being generous? That's a big success that needs to be recognized.

READ:

In 1 Samuel 17, we discover the story about David and Goliath. It's a good win for David, but if you keep reading through 1 Samuel, you will see that he also had failures as well as a few more successes in his life. Think about what that looks like for you.

SECTION 2

GROWING IN FAITH

It's been a whole bunch of years since I was a freshman. I remember that I really didn't have a good understanding of my faith journey. Part of it was my fault. I looked to youth group mostly as my social outlet and a place where my friends and I just hung out. Part of it was my youth leaders' fault because they did a great job of loving me but didn't really put a lot of time into asking me hard questions and pushing me to think about what I believed. I was also pretty immature and not ready for much growth. Fortunately for me, I simply stayed consistent and never missed youth group or church. My growth took place over a long chunk of time as I just slowly became more and more connected to God.

Your story might be totally different. You may be stepping into ninth grade with a pretty solid foundation of faith and a good understanding about how a relationship with Jesus is impacting your life. But there is a high probability that you are somewhere in between that scenario and where I was. I want you to know that where you are is totally OK. God meets us where we are, and we don't have to get to any sort of spiritual place before God shows up in our lives. The key issue is being willing to grow. Maybe your growth will come from consistently going to youth group. Maybe it will come from something different. I've talked to people who say a specific camp, a retreat, or even a testimony put them in a place where growth started. I can't answer the question of what it will take for you, but I can help you to ask questions, take some action, and experiment with what may be the catalyst for your growth.

№ 11 HOW DO YOU CONNECT WITH GOD?

Connecting with God can be difficult. Maybe your youth pastor, parents, or friends seem to have something that you don't. That might bring up questions about whether or not God really exists or makes a difference or wants a vibrant relationship with you. I want you to know that you are not alone. A lot of people have been in the exact same place as you. Many adults go through those kinds of questions and struggles, too. But here's the deal: It may just be that you haven't figured out the best way for *you* to connect with God. For a long time I tried to get up early to read my Bible and pray. And guess what? I was horrible at it. I just couldn't be disciplined enough to do it. It wasn't until I figured out much later in life that I needed to look for God in nature that I discovered how to best connect. Going on walks and getting out into the beauty that God created is the best way for me to really connect. And I still don't do it enough. There are tons of ways of connecting with God: Bible reading, praying, walking in nature, singing or listening to worship music, serving others, practicing silence, fasting, and more.

THINK ABOUT:

1. What's one way that you feel like you connect best with God?

2. What are some ways that you feel like you don't connect with God? Why?

3. What does "connecting with God" even mean to you? How do you know if you have or haven't connected with God?

4. For you, how important is having a regular time with God?

THE WORLD THINKS:

Connecting with things or beings you can't see is weird. Are you going to be a Christian who carries around a big Bible all the time? I don't even understand why you would be even interested in "connecting" anyway. Doesn't Christianity end up only being a list of do's and don'ts? Why would you want to connect with anything that tells you that you can't do the things you want to do?

ACT:

Try some new ways of connecting with God this week. Go on a walk and look around at nature. Sit somewhere quiet and just listen. Take a journal and write out your prayers. Get up early and watch the sunrise. Create something using clay or paint. There are so many different ways of connecting with God, and I believe you will benefit from trying some that are new for you.

READ:

Mark 1:35, Luke 5:16, and John 6:15 — Jesus regularly spent time alone

NO. 12 DOES YOUR CHURCH HELP YOU GROW?

I mentioned in the introduction to this section that my church didn't really help me grow when I was younger. That may not be a truly accurate statement because I'm sure my lack of growth also had something to do with not wanting it. But I do think my youth group enabled me to stay stagnant. You may have a church you really like, feel connected to what happens there, and be challenged by what you hear. You may also have exactly the opposite experience. In my case, my youth group was a hugely important part of my life. My youth pastor was a volunteer. He and the other leaders had great hearts, and I totally felt loved there. But I didn't often hear the name of Jesus or any sort of a plan for growing closer to him. We sang songs, I went to worship services, and I attended every retreat and camp we had. But it just wasn't the place where my growth happened. For me that was at a different church's youth retreat where a friend's dad asked me if I knew Jesus and then explained everything to me. That's when it felt real for the first time.

THINK ABOUT:

1. How does your church/youth group help you grow?

2. What are some specific examples of growth that came from attending or serving at church?

3. Have there been moments where going to church and youth group just felt like a waste of time? Why or why not?

4. How do you think your church could better help you grow? Be specific in your answer.

THE WORLD THINKS:

Church is a waste of time. You'd be better off sleeping in on Sunday mornings and figuring out on your own what you should believe. Going somewhere and having someone tell you what you should believe isn't right. You need freedom and space. Church is a bunch of old people who have nothing better to do. It's all just a bunch of rules, anyway.

ACT:

Want to try something really out of the ordinary this week? Go to a different church and check it out. Go by yourself or with a friend, and see what happens at another congregation. Or find a different youth group and compare it to yours. How do they interact and talk to each other? Find the pastor or youth leader and ask them to give you a brief description of what they are trying to accomplish with students.

READ:

Read Acts 2 — a great picture of the early church and how Christ-followers lived their lives

№13 WHAT HOLDS BACK YOUR GROWTH?

Want to know what held back my growth? It was girls. I liked them a lot, and at youth group I spent more time making sure I was sitting next to the right one than I did anything else. And at camps and retreats I focused a lot of attention on getting to know new ones. In our middle school group now, we call this the "love bug" and it shows up pretty often. You might have something similar holding you back—or something totally different. It could be as simple as year-round soccer or baseball practice that limits your ability to go to youth group. It might be parents who don't want to drive you to church. It could be more serious like an addiction you are struggling with or a home filled with chaos. I realize friends have a lot to do with this, too. They are so important and maybe some of them don't care about faith. Lots of factors can limit your growth. Your job is to figure out how to minimize them.

THINK ABOUT:

1. How important is your faith to you right now? What evidence in your life would confirm your answer?

2. What things right now are holding back your growth?

3. What are some ways you can overcome some of those obstacles?

4. How do you need help in order to grow?

THE WORLD THINKS:

I tried that church thing and it didn't work for me, so I quit. I went to youth group all of middle school and I just grew out of it. I don't have a need for God right now. Maybe when I'm older and have kids of my own I'll go back. I want them to have a foundation, at least, but I don't think it's particularly relevant in my life right now. Besides, the Bible was written so many years ago—how could it possibly relate to high school now?

ACT:

OK, time for something totally different. Find a local Christian ministry that serves people, such as a food pantry or a homeless shelter. Go there and serve. If you have a small group or just an adult you trust, take them with you. Experience what that ministry does, and see the responses of the people they are serving. Maybe this will shake up your world a little bit. Ask the leaders in that ministry why they do what they do.

READ:

Matthew 14:24-33

№14 WHO ARE YOUR IDOLS?

All of us have idols in our lives. This will make me sound totally lame, but growing up I wanted to be one of the Hardy Boys (yes, I realize you probably have no idea who they are). I read books about these guys, and I thought being a young investigator flying all over the world solving mysteries sounded really cool. Later I thought I wanted to be a TV star. I idolized a lot of things, too. I loved cool computers and technology stuff (yes, I am a bit of geek). I idolized people who were at the cutting edge of making tons of money and who had a lot of power. Maybe you are more into athletics and you idolize certain sports figures. Image is a huge idol that many of us struggle with. We want to look a certain way or be a certain type of person. We have pictures of pop stars, actors, and models hanging on our walls—people that we wish we could be more like.

THINK ABOUT:

1. What three people do you most idolize—and why?

2. Is it wrong to have idols? Why or why not?

3. What are some differences between having an idol and having a role model?

THE WORLD THINKS:

Your goal should be to become the idol everyone wants to be like. If you just eat less, you'll be so pretty. If you work harder to be the starting quarterback, everyone will love you. Spend all your time focusing on things that matter, such as money, fame, and popularity. These are the things that really count.

ACT:

It's not wrong to have things you really like. In fact, God created us to have specific talents, desires, and free will. God actually takes delight when we use the gifts he's given us. But we create problems when we put those things before God. Put a rubber band around your wrist; every time you see it, pray that nothing you love would become an idol that you place higher than God.

READ:

Exodus 20:4 and Psalm 39:11

NO. 15 HOW CAN YOU SET THE RIGHT PATTERNS?

I'm not too proud to admit that I often fail at setting good patterns. I'm really good at setting bad ones, though. Somehow it just seems easier to keep doing the things I shouldn't do instead of doing the right things. I remember a time many years ago when I had decided with a friend that we were going to get up every day during the summer and go running on the beach at 7 a.m. The first day was a piece of cake. I woke up easily and was out the door as soon as he got to my house. The problem was the second day. I was sore and couldn't get out of bed. My summer of running lasted exactly one day. Now that I'm a little bit older I find it just as hard. I can stay committed to something just as long as life is simple and easy, but throw a wrench into my plans and it's so easy to stop doing things. Unfortunately, setting good patterns in our faith can be just as challenging. I mentioned before that I hardly ever missed church or youth group growing up. That was a good pattern for me and probably a big part of why I ended up a youth pastor today. It was just "something I did," but it was part of the rhythm of my life that I did every week.

THINK ABOUT:

1. What are some healthy patterns you have in your life right now?

2. What are some unhealthy patterns you might feel stuck in right now?

3. How can you set good patterns in your faith walk that you will be able to follow?

4. What is one pattern you would like to set for your faith?

THE WORLD THINKS:

Please, you're only a freshman in high school. You don't need to waste your time setting patterns right now. Do what feels right and good to you, and don't worry about anything else. You'll have time later on to figure out what you are supposed to do.

ACT:

I hope that when you went through the questions above, you answered truthfully about the pattern you want to set for your faith. The goal from this thought is for you to figure out what that pattern is and then tell three people about it. Write it on a piece of paper and stick it on your bathroom mirror. Put it on a note card and stick it in your binder for school. Do everything you can to help make that thing stick.

READ:

John 13:12-17

NO.16 WHAT DO YOU DO WHEN YOU FAIL?

Failure is something I'm really good at. I have a whole bunch of failure stories from my life. The real question, though, isn't how often we fail but what we do when failure happens. I'll be honest and say that I generally handle it pretty poorly. My go-to method for dealing with it is depression and isolation. (Yeah, I hope you aren't like me in this area.) I think over the years I've gotten better at recognizing this tendency, but it's still relatively prevalent. As a longtime youth pastor, I have a pretty good antenna for when students have struggled and failed with something. I see a lot of you disappearing from church. Someone told me once that they were too ashamed to come to church because of what they had done. I get it. It's difficult and you want to run and hide. I already admitted that's what I do. But it's not healthy. Those of us who work in youth ministry want you to know that when you fail, you need to believe that we are still here with arms open and that we won't love and care for you any differently. So the next time you are struggling or have failed in some area, don't hide or disappear. I'm talking to you (and myself).

THINK ABOUT:

1. What is your go-to response when you struggle or fail at something? Give a specific example.

2. How do you think God sees you when you fail? Why do you believe God sees you this way?

3. What are some ways that you can use your youth group, adult mentors, or friends to help you not fail—or to help you learn how to get back on your feet after you fail?

THE WORLD THINKS:

You are dirty. If you fail, you are worthless and really shouldn't walk inside the doors of a church. It would be better if you didn't come and taint everyone with your unworthiness.

ACT:

Forgiveness can be something that is incredibly hard to give. Chances are good that in the 14 or 15 years you've been alive, someone has hurt you and has failed in your eyes. What if you took a moment to forgive that person? It might be really hard to do. I want to push you to think about failure and forgiveness. One of the reasons we have a hard time believing that God forgives is because we have trouble doing it. So call, write a note, send an email or a social media message, and tell someone that you forgive him or her.

READ:

Acts 2:38, Acts 10:43, and Ephesians 1:7

№ 17 HOW DO YOU MAKE CHOICES?

Maybe you haven't had to make a lot of tough choices yet in your life. Or the choices you have made don't feel like they've been particularly difficult. Guess what? They'll get harder. I don't want to discourage you, but learning to make tough choices is one of those things you must do. Here's a really tough choice I once had to make: I was engaged to marry a woman I thought I was *the* one. I felt like God had brought her into my life and she was perfect. But after we'd been engaged for a few months, I started having doubts. Sometimes doubts can be healthy and helpful, and in this case I felt like God used them to help me make the most difficult choice of my life. I knew that walking away from that relationship was going to cause all kinds of difficulties in my life. I lost friends. I was living in a different state from where I grew up. I had to find a new church. My core of who I was felt damaged, as I had to reimagine my future. That was a tough decision, but ultimately it was the right one. I can't even imagine what life would have been like had I not made it. God is so good and ultimately brought me the most amazing wife, and we have incredible kids. Decisions are tough and you will be faced with a lot of them in life, so be ready.

THINK ABOUT:

1. What's the hardest decision you've had to make?

2. Where do you look for answers when you have to make tough decisions?

3. How do you know which decision is right?

4. Which specific people can help you make good, wise, right decisions?

THE WORLD THINKS:

Just go with what feels right. Don't worry if something was wrong; just get out of it and do something else. Don't worry about other people's feelings; you are the center of your own universe, so all you have to do is make the right decisions for yourself.

ACT:

Ask someone about a tough decision they've made and how they handled it. Find an adult—a youth worker, parent, teacher, or coach—and ask them about the hardest decision they have made and what they learned from that experience.

READ:

Proverbs 16:33, John 8:16, and Philippians 4:6-7

№.18 WHAT ABOUT YOUR FRIENDS?

Friends are incredibly important. When I was in high school, I had a group of close friends. We did a ton together, and they were a big part of my life. My church wasn't very big, and I considered most everyone in my youth group to be a friend. They were a big part of life. But my youth group wasn't always a source of spiritual growth for me. In fact, many friends from youth group were the same ones that I saw at parties on the weekends. I made pretty good choices for much of high school and college; my friends didn't cause me to stumble too much. But it was always a temptation and a struggle because I knew that they wouldn't question or judge anything I did. But I would never have been able to walk away from my friends. You might hear at some point in your life that if you want to make better decisions, you have to surround yourself with people who make good decisions. The problem is that none of us wants to walk away from our friends because we don't want to be alone. Lots here to think about.

THINK ABOUT:

1. How have your friends helped you to grow—or have they?

2. Are your friends doing things that you don't want to get caught up in? If so, how are you handling these situations?

3. How have you lost friends? How did that make you feel?

4. If you have any friends who aren't followers of Jesus, what do you as a Christ-follower believe is your responsibility to them?

THE WORLD THINKS:

The most important people in your life are your friends. They are more important than your parents or anyone else. Don't do anything that will cause your friendships to end. Your friends have your back and will always be there for you.

ACT:

What if you tried to actively reach out to people at your school who don't appear to have any friends? I know that in youth ministry we often talk about the kid who has no one to sit next to at lunch, but what if you really did that? How might you impact someone that feels lonely if you reached out to him or her? It doesn't have to be lunch. Sometimes just a simple smile to someone who doesn't often receive one will make a huge difference.

READ:

1 Samuel 18:3

NO.19 WHAT HAPPENS WHEN YOU GET BUSY?

Life gets busy. I don't know about you, but I feel the pressure to always be doing *something*. You're just starting high school and might be handling sports, clubs, jobs, homework, youth group, family stuff, and more. It's a whole new thing in ninth grade with so much pressure and responsibility. It's hard. I tried convincing myself for a long time that I was better and more worthy when I was involved in many things at the same time. I don't have any clue how I successfully managed it all without a smartphone and online calendar! But I did, and I was able to mostly do everything right. Unfortunately for me, there were the moments when it just felt like everything I was doing had a major project, due date, game, or need all at the same time. Those moments were when I often crashed and got sick. Or I would be good all week long and then not be able to get out of bed on the weekends. I was horrible at balancing priorities because everything just seemed important.

THINK ABOUT:

1. When you get busy, how do you prioritize everything you need to do?

2. What things are you currently doing that you wish you could just quit?

3. How pressured do you feel by your parents to do things?

4. When you get stressed, what is your usual response?

THE WORLD THINKS:

If you don't get involved in everything you possible can as a freshman and build your résumé, you will never get into the college you want. You have to fill your schedule with everything so that you will appear "well rounded" and look like the kind of student that a college wants to accept. Busyness is a great thing and will eventually lead you to be successful in life.

ACT:

Grab a sheet of paper, and in one column write down everything you are currently doing and the amount of time you think it takes you each week. In another column write down some things that you wish you could do but you just can't seem to find time to do. Now take this list and pray over it. Ask God to direct you to which things you are supposed to be doing and which things you maybe should cut. Seek guidance for things you wish you had time to do.

READ:

Ecclesiastes 3:1-8

NO. 20 DO YOU APPRECIATE THE IMPACT OF YOUR WORDS?

Words. We use a ton of them every day. Many are spoken, but a lot are texted or typed on websites. We communicate all kinds of messages through what we say, how we say it, and what we don't say. One thing I have always had trouble with was slowing down the words coming out of my mouth and thinking about what I'm saying before I actually say it. I've hurt people with words. I have hurt family and friends. We have so much power when we say things. I think about how news media use politicians' "sound bites" over and over from long speeches the candidates give—trying to simplify everything into just a few words. You might find that when you come home from school someone (likely a parent) will ask you how you day went. You might be inclined to just say "fine" and try to leave it at that. I'm guessing, though, that the person asking you actually does care how your day went—and if you had a difficult one, they want to really know about it.

THINK ABOUT:

1. How have your words hurt someone? How have another person's words hurt you?

2. What are some things that have been said to you that have encouraged you?

3. Do you have conversations with your parents where you share how you are really doing? Why or why not?

THE WORLD THINKS:

People need to have thicker skin. If they can't take the truth, then that's their problem and not yours. Say whatever you think, and if other people can't handle it, it's not your fault.

ACT:

What would your day look like if you decided to listen instead of talk? I challenge you to take an entire school day and not talk unless you have to. So if a teacher asks you a question, answer it, but with other people try to limit your talking to almost nothing. Don't tell people what you are doing. See if they notice. You will probably be surprised at the responses you receive if you are acting quiet.

READ:

Job 6:24, Psalm 34:8, Ecclesiastes 9:17, James 1:26, and James 3:5

SECTION 3

WHERE IS JESUS...

547 548 549

You've now made it through 20 devotions, and I hope you are being challenged and encouraged by everything you have read and all the questions you've answered. These next 10 devotions tackle the question "Where is Jesus?" Just so you understand, though, I'm asking the question but not trying to give you an answer. One thing I've learned over the years is that we all need to be accepted for where we are, not where someone else wants us to be. That's why I want you to answer the question for yourself. If you look back to the cover of this book, you'll see that the subtitle for this book is "Making faith your priority." That's what I really want you to think about in the last third of this book.

№.21 ...IN YOUR RELATIONSHIPS?

I think relationships are much harder now than when I was growing up. Back in my day (that sounds old) we didn't have cell phones, Internet, text messaging, chat rooms, or anything like that. At school, guys could see their girlfriends and girls could see their boyfriends, but then we went home and that was it (other than using the phone or occasionally hanging out). Now you have the ability to stay connected to your significant other almost 24 hours a day if you want. I can't even imagine what it would have been like for me in high school if I'd had that opportunity. I think it wouldn't have been good because of the way a relationship could go deep quickly if I had no downtime from that person. It would be so easy to get so close so quick. And as an adult, I totally fail enough at having to explain what I mean in a text message. So I pray for you as you enter into this crazy dating world with social media and communication being so easy. Because relationships can gain this depth so quickly, it becomes even harder to make sure to maintain a healthy dialogue with Jesus about what you should be doing. It's almost as if you have to be really careful because before you know it, you are in a serious relationship and you may have not really talked to Jesus about it first. So I'm praying for you.

THINK ABOUT:

1. How do you make decisions about relationships?

2. What things are important to you when you think about dating?

3. What are specific ways you can involve your faith in your dating?

4. Have you ever felt like things were moving too fast in a dating relationship? How can you stop that from happening?

THE WORLD THINKS:

Just jump in and date whoever you want. It's all casual, right? You should "try before you buy"—and consider trying out a lot. Don't worry about consequences now because you are young.

ACT:

What if you put together a "group date" for some friends? Get some guys and girls together to do something fun with no expectations, pressure, or drama. You might find this is a totally healthy and easier way to get to know people.

READ:

John 15:13, 1 Corinthians 13:4-8, and Ephesians 4:2-3

NO.22 ...IN YOUR FUTURE?

You probably have some dreams about what you would like to see happen in your future. Maybe you have been thinking about this for a long time and you have a path pretty well mapped out. Or you might be totally the opposite: no clue about what you want to do. Well, some good news: Both are OK. A lot of us have dreams. I went to college originally as a computer science major. I realized pretty quickly that wasn't where my gifts were. After flirting with law school, I worked as a teacher for a while before finally becoming a youth pastor. It's funny now to look back over my journey and see the real, distinct handprint of Jesus pushing me toward working in the church with teenagers. I can see it in so many places. Jesus will lead if you allow him the chance. As a freshman, it might not feel like you have to worry about the future too much. The reality is that you probably don't. Take some time to just enjoy and be yourself. But when you are ready, ask Jesus to lead.

THINK ABOUT:

1. If you had to choose a career right now, what would you pick—and why?

2. What talents and skills do you think God has given you?

3. Who are some people in your life you can ask for help in figuring this out?

4. Do you think God has one plan for you, or are there multiple things you could try?

THE WORLD THINKS:

You have to figure this out now. Just pick the job that you think is going to make you the most money so that you are happy—because that's what really matters. The only person who cares about your future and can make things happen is you. So you need to have a plan and do it.

ACT:

Find an older Christian person in your world that you can go to lunch with and ask them to share with you how they saw Jesus leading them into their future. See what they can tell you about the path they traveled. Ask them what it was like if they tried to do it alone. Where did they finally figure it out?

READ:

Psalm 33:11, Proverbs 19:21, and Jeremiah 29:11

№.23 ...IN YOUR FAMILY?

You might have a family that is all about going to church and being involved. Or you might have the opposite. I had both experiences growing up. For a big season my family was very active and involved in church. I never missed vacation Bible school or any other thing. My family was always there. We prayed at meals, and it felt like our faith was important. Then some things changed and I ended up being the only one who still went to church. We still prayed at dinner, but Jesus sort of stopped being a part of our lives. I'll be honest: It makes me kind of sad. Since you are reading this devotional book, I'm going to guess that Jesus is kind of important to you and maybe to your family, too. But life is busy and there is always a ton of pressure. No one is perfect. At times you might see in your family things that don't really look like they involve Jesus. The Bible is full of stories of somewhat wacky families that still ended up following the Lord in their own way. I hope you have great examples from your parents, but if you don't, maybe you are called to be that example for them or other family members.

THINK ABOUT:

1. What place or role does Jesus have in your family?

2. How important do you think faith is to your parents?

3. What kinds of conversations do you have about Jesus with your family members?

THE WORLD THINKS:

Families are so messed up; you shouldn't put too much hope in your family, anyway. And really, Jesus doesn't have much to do with your family. Just go to church a couple of times each year at Christmas and Easter and you'll have done your part.

ACT:

Do you know your family's faith history? There may be parts of the story you know, but what about the whole of it? This week, ask your parents to tell you their story of faith. We often call this a "testimony." Find out why faith is important (or not) to your parents. How has it impacted decisions they've made?

READ:

Psalm 22:27 and Acts 10:2

№.24 ...IN THE WORLD?

You might not see Jesus in the world very much. He often isn't someone we spend a lot of time looking for. Maybe around Christmas or Easter you'll see Jesus on the cover of some magazine. Or you'll hear him mentioned if something controversial paints Jesus in a bad light. But in the daily reality of a ninth-grader, you may not see him. Unless, of course, you take time to really look. But how you look is a great question. Sure, it would be easy if Jesus was walking around today and performing miracles on the streets. That would be on TV and the Internet almost immediately. But it doesn't work like that. Often we have to look at Jesus working "through" people. Maybe that's the place to start.

THINK ABOUT:

1. How do you see Jesus in the world today?

2. Who can you look to that Jesus is working through?

3. When do you know that Jesus is at work?

THE WORLD THINKS:

Jesus is dead. That's what happened on the cross. He doesn't have a place in the world today. You people who believe that have issues. You need something you can't find on your own so you try to act like Jesus has some sort of place now. We're tired of you Christians acting like it matters. It doesn't. We tolerate all the hype around Christmas and Easter and we might even go to your church because our parents want us to, but we don't believe any of it.

ACT:

Today's questions included one asking whom you can see Jesus working through. You might not have had an answer. But keep looking into this. With some friends or a small group, find a ministry that is caring for people in your town. Go spend an afternoon helping them out. See how they work and what they do. Ask people there why they are doing what they do. You'll probably hear a lot about Jesus.

READ:

Matthew 25:34-46

№.25 ...IN YOUR STRUGGLES?

I can still remember a lot of the struggles I went through in ninth grade. I wasn't exactly the most popular kid at school. Middle school had been hard, and I really just wanted to try and hide and blend in and not get involved in too much. I was shy; I had only a few friends. In my opinion it was a tough life. As I got older it got better, but I also had to deal with more struggles. I don't know what you are wrestling with right now. My prayer is that you aren't struggling with any major issues. But the reality is you might be—and if not now, then you likely will at some point. We all probably wish that we had a magical "Jesus button" that we could press when we struggle—if we made a really bad decision, pressing that button would make all things right. We could start over and act as if it didn't ever happen. Unfortunately, both you and I know that Jesus doesn't work like that. But I wonder if we really fully understand how he *does* work? I hope you take some time to pray, think through, and talk about this with people who are maybe a little further along on this journey than you.

THINK ABOUT:

1. Do you think Jesus cares about your struggles? Why or why not?

2. How do you think Jesus enters into our issues with us?

3. Are there people in your life that you feel you can go to when you are struggling with something?

4. What is your go-to response when you find yourself struggling with something?

THE WORLD THINKS:

You are on your own. You got yourself into this mess, and you'll have to get yourself out of it. It's no one's problem but your own. Good luck with that, and please don't let your issues affect us. Everyone has problems. You'll get over it. Jesus doesn't care about you. Your problems are so small compared to major things happening in the world. If there really were a Jesus, he'd focus on those things not you.

ACT:

Time to put a little research hat on. Look up "miracles" on the Internet and filter through stories looking for Jesus today. You are probably going to be a little bit surprised at how many miracles people believe are still happening right now. Then go ask some people you trust how Jesus was a part of their struggles. Think about what they say.

READ:

Romans 15:30 and Ephesians 6:12

ᴺᴼ·26 ...IN YOUR DOUBTS?

I'm going to guess that every once in a while you struggle with believing certain things. It might be as simple as having no idea how you are going to make a deadline, pass a test, or fix a broken friendship. In your faith you may wonder if this whole "Jesus, God, and the Bible" thing is real. You feel like you are putting a whole bunch of energy and effort into something that might be a total lie. That's a hard place to be because doubt puts a huge damper on everything. It's almost like it removes the color from a picture. You may really struggle when you doubt. It may be something that is hard for you because it causes you to question yourself and to wonder what your problem is. I have some hope for you, though: Doubt is good. Jesus isn't afraid of your doubts. And in the church we aren't scared of your doubts either. We want you to have the freedom to wrestle through things and work stuff out for yourself. Sure, we want to help you and free you from doubt, but we also want to sit with you while you experience it. Youth workers are not scared of your doubt and questions. We want you to have the freedom to express how you really feel. I trust this gives you some hope and encouragement.

THINK ABOUT:

1. What are some of your doubts about Christianity?

2. How do you feel when you have doubts?

3. Where do you look for answers?

THE WORLD THINKS:

Skepticism and cynicism are good. Don't get sucked into believing things that aren't true and can't be proved. Don't trust people, because you'll just get hurt. The Bible is an outdated book written by too many people a long time ago. You can't trust what it says in there anyway.

ACT:

Make a list of things you doubt about faith. Let the list be as long as you need it to be. Then start asking people about those doubts. Find a youth worker, parent, or friend and ask them to explain things to you. You may still have doubts, but their answers likely will help you.

READ:

Luke 24:38, John 20:27, and Jude 1:22

ꜰᴼ·27 ...IN YOUR SCHOOL?

A couple of years ago, I was a youth pastor in a church in Texas. One day a student who was fairly connected to our church committed suicide. A whole bunch of youth pastors all ended up at school that day to be with students. We were welcomed in by people on the school staff, who knew that our presence was a good thing. Unfortunately, this isn't such a common thing. Often there is a major separation between church and school, and it is difficult for us to be where you are. I'm pretty convinced that Jesus wants to have something to do with your school. I've found over the years that Jesus has a place in the spots that are most important to us, the spots where we spend a lot of time. I'm not sure what that looks like at your school. Maybe some Bible studies or clubs meet at your school. Young Life, the Fellowship of Christian Athletes, and other groups have been meeting on school campuses for a long time. Your school likely even has some Christian teachers, too.

THINK ABOUT:

1. What types of Christian clubs or groups are at your school?

2. What are some ways you could share Jesus with people at school?

3. How do you think Jesus might want to be at your school?

THE WORLD THINKS:

There is a reason we have a separation of church and state; Jesus shouldn't be in our schools. But if we are going to let him and Christians in, we have to open up the door to everyone. And we have to make sure to not offend anyone.

ACT:

Go to school and see what types of Christian clubs or activities exist. Check them out and see if any of them meet your need right now. Yes, I remember you are a freshman and you might not know what your need is. Go anyway.

READ:

John 8:12 and John 18:20

№28 ...IN YOUR PAIN?

I went through a really difficult season in my life when I was younger. My family was going through a roller coaster ride of dysfunction, and my parents weren't living together. I felt as if my whole foundation of life had suddenly disappeared, and I had no clue how to function in this new normal. I felt like my friends really didn't understand how bad I was hurting, and the answers they were giving me just weren't helpful. It was so hard, and I was completely unprepared. I remember days when I only left my room a few times. I dived into books to try to experience a different reality and to mask the pain I felt. It lasted for a long time. One day I couldn't take it anymore, and I just went to a friend's house to talk. I ended up lying on his floor crying while he and a couple of other people prayed for me. This was the beginning of healing because I was allowing Jesus to meet me in the pain I was feeling. I don't know what kind of pain you might be experiencing now. The only thing I can say is that Jesus absolutely wants to be with us in our pain.

THINK ABOUT:

1. How do you respond to pain?

2. Have you had any situations of pain that you felt Jesus was able to help you with?

3. How have you been able to help other people who are experiencing pain?

THE WORLD THINKS:

Pain is just something you have to suck up and deal with. Everyone experiences pain. Everyone hurts. Everyone gets over it. Just figure out how to do it on your own. No one can really help you through it. It's up to you.

ACT:

There might be a homeless shelter or food pantry/kitchen in your town. Get together with some other people and see if you can go and serve. As you serve, see if you can talk to the people who work there and are being served there, and listen to them share how they find help. If it is a Christian ministry, ask them about how Jesus meets them in their pain. The answers they share may give you insight to better know how Jesus will meet you in your pain.

READ:

Psalm 69:29, John 16:19-22, and Revelation 21:4

ℕ⒪·29 ...IN YOUR FEARS?

I fell once. I was on a youth group trip in the mountains of Washington. I'm pretty sure I was a freshman at the time. We were hiking in the summer, and from our camp we could see a snowfield several hundred feet above us. A couple of friends and I decided to hike up and play in the snow. It was really steep and the footing was treacherous. Near the top of the snowfield I slipped and started sliding really fast down the face of it. There was a major crevice near the bottom, and I was convinced I was going to fall in it. Stuck in the snow were a whole bunch of rocks that had fallen in. I tried using these as handholds to stop. Right before the crevice, my strategy worked and I jerked to a stop. I remember just lying there grateful for that rock in my hand. I was so scared and shaky. I remember thinking how glad I was that Jesus had put that rock there so I could grab it. Yes, I believe Jesus put that rock there. I believe he had a bigger purpose for me, and in that moment of being terrified he was with me in fear. I'm guessing your fear is probably something totally different from mine. You may have a harder time seeing how Jesus will be there for you. I hope, though, that through the questions below and the action idea you will see more how Jesus might step into your fears with you.

THINK ABOUT:

1. What is something you are totally afraid of?

2. How might Jesus enter into that fear with you?

3. What are some ways you can confront or overcome some of your fears?

4. If fear wasn't an issue at all, what's one thing you wish you could try?

THE WORLD THINKS:

You're only a freshman. What do you know about fear? The things you are afraid of are silly compared to other people. And what does Jesus have to do with your fears? The only way you will overcome anything is by being completely like a stone. You can't let anything get to you. Fear is failure.

ACT:

One thing we can do to overcome our fears is to allow ourselves to experience just a little bit of them at a time. So if you are afraid to speak in front of people, sneak into the auditorium and get on the stage and talk when the room is empty. Or practice what you would say to that girl or guy you want to ask to the homecoming dance. Figure out one fear that you identified above and see what you can do to practice overcoming a little of it.

READ:

Joshua 1:6-9

ℕ.30 ...IN YOUR PRIORITIES?

One thing you will face as a freshman is how to prioritize things in your life. You have the possibility of doing so many things and trying to figure out which is best, but it is sometimes really difficult. I once had a ninth-grade guy in my youth group who was the kid that I often hoped wouldn't show up. He would always distract the group and make it really difficult for us to get anything done. But he never missed. His sophomore year he was playing water polo and could only be at our small group for about a half-hour each Wednesday. He always rushed to be with us. He made it a huge priority. I got to watch this kid who drove me nuts turn into a kid who loved Jesus so much that every part of his life and all of his decisions were influenced by his faith. And then a few years ago he asked me to perform his wedding, and I had the opportunity to share about how proud I was about how he made his priorities.

THINK ABOUT:

1. How important right now is your faith to you?

2. When you have to make important decisions, what do you do?

3. Do you think Jesus cares about the choices you make? How and why?

THE WORLD THINKS:

Your priority needs to be making sure you get a great job and make lots of money so you can have a happy life. Focus on yourself because ultimately you are the only one who cares about you. Faith is something that you can come back to when you get older.

ACT:

Go find someone you respect and ask that person how he or she made faith a priority in life. Ask them how they made tough decisions and how they feel Jesus was a part of those choices. See if they will tell you about any times they failed to prioritize their faith and how that felt.

READ:

Luke 22:32 and 1 Corinthians 2:1-5

FOLLOW-UP

You've just gone through 30 devotions aimed at helping you make your faith a priority this first year of high school. I know it probably wasn't always easy. There are a lot of competing things that you could be doing, and it can be difficult to focus on something like this.

But you've made it. You've finished. You have done something significant, and you can feel proud of that.

Maybe you did this with your small group leader or your youth group. I hope that the discussions were helpful and that thinking about how the world might respond was a good reminder. The action steps were aimed at getting you doing things that would reinforce decisions you were making.

Well done. I hope you are looking forward to your sophomore year of high school. In the next book we will be encouraging you to "Step into Maturity." I believe it will also be a great experience!

-Lars